From Here to There:
Uneven Steps
Marking Time

CLEMENT WHITE

authorHOUSE®

AuthorHouse™
1663 Liberty Drive
Bloomington, IN 47403
www.authorhouse.com
Phone: 1 (800) 839-8640

Published by AuthorHouse 12/14/2017

ISBN: 978-1-5462-1862-3 (sc)
ISBN: 978-1-5462-1861-6 (hc)
ISBN: 978-1-5462-1860-9 (e)

Library of Congress Control Number: 2017918042

Print information available on the last page.

In Memory of: MARJORIE-MARGARITA
ASTA WHITE STEVENS—
JEANNETTE SMITH WHITE

FOR EDGAR LAKE, PROLIFIC WRITER, SCHOLAR, FRIEND

FOR BERNICE LOUISE HEYLIGER.
MY BELOVED TEACHER AND COUSIN

Contents

PART II

Acknowledgements

Endless thanks to my wife, Dr. Jeannette Smith White, who continues to inspire me. I received constant encouragement and support from her. To our children, Sekou "Chike" and Asha, grandsons, Amari, and Ahsir and granddaughter Avani ("mi princesa") you mean everything to me.

To my mother, Marjorie, "Miss Maggie", so much thanks for uncompromising, unconditional support; now even as her work on earth was ended on October 10, 2014, I know that she will continue to guide and inspire me; so remarkable a woman, mother, and human being she was. She never attended school nor ever read a book but was my first teacher.

Ana Cecilia Rosado thanks for your years of friendship. To Marta Rodríguez Galán for many years of support.

To my sister Cheryl A. White, because of your dedication to our mother, I was able to continue writing. I recognize and appreciate your sacrifice and dedication to our beloved mother. Your rewards will be great! No amount of words can explain what you have done for our family.

To fellow and sister writers Habib Tiwoni, Dr. Gilbert Sprauve, Elaine Warren Jacobs, Dr. Vincent Cooper, Daisy Holder, Dr. Ruby Simmonds, Larry Sewer, Tregenza Roach and the prolific Dr. Simon B. Jones Hendrickson, Edgar Lake and Richard Scharader, you are an inspiration to all Virgin Islands writers; your works have served as literary models over the years. Edgar, you are a brilliant scholar whose advice and guidance have been instrumental in my literary career. Miss Ruth Thomas, your guidance has made a difference in my life and in the lives of generations of Virgin Islanders.

To my colleagues Mario Trubiano, Susana de los Heros, and Tomás Morín— Gracias por todo el apoyo. Karla Crispín, thanks for all your technical advice and support. Ms Fiolina Mills, thank you so much for your Spanish lessons and guidance,

Shirlene Williams Lee from the very beginning in the 1960's you played a pivotal role in the transcription of my work, typing my manuscripts with your inimitable professionalism and expertise. Words are insufficient to express my gratitude to you. Critic, poet, analyst, sounding board, artist, photographer, designer, and more importantly, friend—from the first grade at the extraordinary Dober School until now! You have been there every step of the way. Everything you do, you do it well. Without your assistance this project would have never been completed.

So much inspiration for this project came from my many years as summer faculty and Faculty Coordinator at the Institute for the Recruitment of Teachers in Andover, Massachusetts (**IRT**). I thank the many students, faculty, administration and staff over the two and a half decades for their motivation and encouragement. Special thanks to my former students at the Institute: Dr. Reginald Wilburn, Curriculum Coordinator (&faculty), Dr. Besenia Rodríguez, Curriculum Coordinator (& faculty). Dr. Alexis Cornelius, Director (&faculty). No less gratitude for Dr. Asabe Poloma, Executive Director (&faculty), Dr. Alexandra Cornelius (former Director & faculty), and Dr. Kelly Wise, founder of the Institute, (former Director, Faculty, and Executive Director).

Mrs. Bernice Louise Heyliger, everyone now knows that without you, I would not be writing anything. Endless thanks and appreciation.

Cover Photography by Shirlene Williams Lee

The poet's eye, in a fine frenzy rolling,
Doth glance from heaven to earth, from earth to heaven;
And as imagination bodies forth
The forms of things unknown, the poet's pen
Turns them to shapes and gives to aery nothing
A local habitation and a name.

William Shakespeare, A Midsummer Night's Dream, Act V, I, 12-17

Introduction

Several years ago I was asked in an interview about my "outline" for writing poetry, and my answer, I suppose, surprised the interviewer: "I have none, but rather I believe that my poetry responds to a call from within me, as natural as Vicente Huidobro was proposing." I vividly remember this response, recalling the Chilean's poet blueprint in his work "Poetic Art."("Arte poética,"1916). I have always felt a sense of liberation reading Huidobro and contemplating the words: "Let the verse be like a key that open a thousand doors." The doors that are opened, I believe, should lead to more views of the world and hopefully some introspection. And none of this should ever preclude artistic creativity and freedom. The idea that poetry is a clearly defined genre has long been discredited and seen as pretext for traditionalists who prefer formulaic representations of expressions. I stay as far as possible from this debate since I am obligated only to the truth emanating from within me.

In 2015 I had the privilege of attending a conference in la Habana Cuba, and was immediately inspired to respond to the muses in the land of José Martí and Nicolás Guillén. Verses written in Spanish are interpreted into English. The poems on Cuba are included in this collection and in **Come Lemme Hea' Yoh Yank Soursap.**

PART I

Uneven Steps To Nowhere

Broken stairs protruding outward
Result of inexact architecture
Zigzagging stairs
destiny unsure
Signaling by their mere style
Guarantees of uneven steps
Proof of lapsing seconds and moments
Lost within the frenzy of designated
Yet unassigned inevitabilities,
Splintered stairs with their
Suggested upward motion in a
Fierce drive to stand still,
Motionless stairs
Still stairs
Still symbolically ascending and descending
In a paradoxical game of confusion,
And illusion
Where contradictory motions
Lay claim to movement control, stairs so fractured
They baffle those using them
As guide,
Unsure stairs
Uneven steps
Quickly moving
Rushing
Nowhere

Inscription

Sobbing sounds awoke me,
unstructured silhouette imbedded
in the wall beckons me
I refused to approach that wall
where countless acts of nature
are repressed by time's coarse hands,
amid sobbing sounds with my name sporadically
echoed,
Dexterity is the name of
nature's cantankerous clock
bearing markers of life's rugged pathways

Sobbing sounds continue to
urge me on,
in an earnest frustrated moment,
a moment of anxiety,
footsteps leading to the wall
create a trail for me to follow
the singular pathway to
the wall with its
tell-tale signs,
The wall that sits motionless
directing all to scale it
in search of
unwritten diaries of unspeakable truths

Un Inspired Muse

The Muses ran wild, laughing,
dancing at the process of creativity
that they promised to encourage,
They danced and smiled, these creatures of
Inventions,
Then turned deadly serious,
no longer serene,
No longer pacific,
The Muses ran wild in directions
undetermined and arbitrary
having seen for themselves the
new creators and
inventors giving birth
to other worlds
The Muses witnessed the birth,
the mothers,
the fathers
the creators
inventors
looked intently at their new offspring
And the Muses, symbols of inspiration,
chafed and squirmed at the thought of the
new creations,
They ran wild, the Muses
and yielded in
spirit to the new creations

and creators
and the contortionists of the New World,
alien to the Muses
with their characteristic trait of inspiration and hope

The Backbone

Tireless mothers, defiant,
yet forgotten,
names obliterated in the midst of the
unforgiving ocean tides,
History labels you obedient
passive
submissive,
clear mischaracterizations,
concoction of *HISstory*
Truth endlessly purged

Pained MOTHERS bitterly aware of
the activities below in the holes
of destruction,
the den of doom,
MOTHERS,
suffering witnesses of
instrumentations of death,
MOTHERS, bearers of life,
Lives snatched before
your eyes,
wretched acts of legality,
A cruel joke enjoyed only by the
pranksters on the boats of hell,
the dungeons, infernos of the
boats of your destiny and
the destiny of yours,
moans

groans
pain,
loss of consciousness in a place of no
conscience
loss of mind
all come together as one
in a unifying scent of degrading perfume
reserved for the woman still desperately
determined to rescue those around her,
headed as she was across the seas to a
glorious life in the Americas

Obamafrica

Obama
President of the Greatest Nation
Stood
At the **Door of No Return**,
And sighed
Emotionally drained by the thought of souls
Sent to death camps
Under the guise of God's love,
Human cargo neatly packaged to be
Bartered
Bargained
Negotiated, haggled
To the winners, possessors of the
Highest value capital,
The President stood in awe of souls
Left behind who were *"spared"*
The arduous journey, their newly concocted names
Omitted arbitrarily from the manifests
Of the souls of the death camp,
Metonymed by the **Door of No Return**,
The President felt the emotion
No other President ever felt
Because Africa runs through and through
His veins,
Inextricably linked to Kenya,
One of Africa's greatest nations and preserver of sacred truths,
Obama spoke truth,
Given wisdom

By the spirits of the departed souls
From the Gorée Island
      Who looked back,
      And there was a tear in the eye of each
      Man
      Woman
      Child,
      A tear for the non-departed,
      Departing nonetheless to the halls of death,
      Those destined to stay
      Shed tears, one for each
      Man
      Woman
      Child
      Shackled in the ships with their own
      Dungeons,
      Safe and
      Secured in the jars of pending death,
      Many tears were shed as brothers
      And sisters,
      Mothers, fathers, locked gazes,
      And we saw the residue tears in the eyes
      Of the only President
      Bold enough to imagine the realities
      Of a sordid history that allows him
      Tangency

The American Refugees

They walk the streets
now called refugees,
strangers in their own land,
a land never really theirs,
rebuffed by policies,
too subtle to unravel,
unspoken rules unchanged by
time

They roam the streets,
the highways,
the byways,
defying destiny
defying the history
that marked them,
defying death
whose pathway
is facilitated by policies
too subtle to pinpoint
unspoken rules of time

Babies crying,
distressed by hunger,
No consciousness of gales,
of strong deadly winds
of breaking levees,
Just tears linked to the
absence of milk,
of food
of sustenance
Mothers, fathers,
once rebuffed by humans
Now pleading to cameras
on behalf of screaming
babes
pleading in the night,
at sunrise,
in vain
as society's unspoken rules once
again
dictate the fate
of those
linked to the country's
refugee camps,
camps formed not by Katrina,
but by traditions' pernicious and
unpardonable ways

*Hurricane Katrina 2005

Darkened The Firmament

Opaque skies overlooking seas
That harbor secrets
So ancient, so real,
Secrets perhaps never to be revealed,
The channels of the seas, their numerous
passageways blocked by the sheer gravity of the secrets
mutter unfamiliar sounds in codes
Telegraphed by the same seas
Laying dormant beneath
the heaven's opaque skies
That bore witness at every point
But could not speak the secrets of the reality
unfolding unabashedly in full view,
The darkened skies,
Once translucent and bright
but now darkened and transformed
By suffocating secrets
and
By the burden of the silence of
History

Swinging Door

Door opened
Inviting you to taste freedom
On the shores of the Americas,
Escape the dungeons,
Dingy quarters,
Suites designed especially
For you
Senegalese
Ghanaian,
Child
Woman
Man,
Who opened the door to
Your *freedom* in lands of strangers,
Of shackles,
Of whips that will intimately
Claim your backs?
Iron brands spelt your name as
"B-E-A-S-T."
Who opened the door,
Gateway to Hades
To spare you the asphyxiating
Confinement in your fortress
in the vessel's bosom
where fresh excrement
is the least of your worries?
The church** above sings praises
To God

"Thank God for whom all blessings flow,"
They raise their voices in unison,
Voices of glorification, more cacophonic
Than the moans blending with them
In the most intense historic moments of torture,
"God bless the child" beams the choir
close enough to
the auction site
as voices of hypocrisy shocked no one
awaiting the torture chamber in the depths,
in the bellows of hell,
Who opened the door, Senegal,
and announced
once and for all:
"No Return?
**[note: There were churches erected above the dungeons]

Door For Invited Guests

Go seek fortune,
go seek fame in the lands
that will save you from eternal
damnation in the dungeons
that still smell
of blood, of gore,
of mutilated souls.
Babies too weak to cry,
Sucking milk of blood from
Diseased breasts

What generous hands opened that gate, Ghana?
Of no negotiation
Of no debate
Of **No Return?**
Pack your bags, lucky ones
Give thanks to the
Selection committee,
Who deemed you sufficiently fit
For the journey, across the waters,
To the Caribbean,
To my Virgin Islands?
Sing along with the choir of doom in the
Church from above

My ancestors, winners of the
Freedom lottery!
Who opened that door at Cape Coast Castle
Where bloodied waters have not
Been totally diluted?
No doubt you bade farewell
Hugged and kissed
My other family, left frozen
In blood
In the dungeons where narratives of
Truths were written

Who guaranteed this voyage, Ghana?
Who opened the door,
Senegal?
Who opened the door, Africa,
And in so doing revealed their humanitarian side?
Sparing you the suffering in the pits of hell,
Assuring your one way trip
To Hades,
While the choir above sang
"Hallelujah" and
"May *God bless the child*!

Inevitability

I think of Kenya
Majestic, regal nation
Unique cultures
Amazing peoples,
Proud and strong
Fighting with might
Against colonialism,
Aimed at appropriating
The nation's traditions and
Cultures,
Kenya, the protagonist of my
Dreams
Imagining being in your presence,
Connecting with what I know
Is somehow connected to me,
Kenya shaking off the weight
Of endless colonial projects
Opting for the protection of its
People, its place
Its customs and cultures,
I think ancestry and move ever
So closer to trying to unravel
The riddles and mysteries of
My own identity
Unsure of history's zigzagged course
In shaping me, in molding me,
In determining me,

I think and envision Kenya
Linked to me
Potential ancestral home in the complicated
Map of history, pinpointing geographical
"truths"
But unable to lay bare the rugged roads
That lead to the origin of other stories
So vibrant, so poignant, so piercing,
Hence I dream of this country
Distant in geographical space from me
But lurking securely in the most
Reserved spaces of my subconscious
Making me a child of Africa
A son of that glorious nation
Rich in ways that I cannot quantify,
I think of Kenya and place myself comfortably
In the security of its bosom.

Catapult

Each present moment historicizes me
I must live the present but I have no choice
But to communicate with the past
Seeking insight, clarity,
Trying to unravel moments that
Offer the most enduring lessons,
Life's soldiers often detest the past
For its immutable pattern,
Its rigid chronology,
Life's subjects condemn the past
For its incompetence
Its impotence
Its indifference
I seek the past, but to get there
I must choose the present with
Its bumpy roads, its scary precipice
Its treacherous side ramps
Unnegotiable mountains and valleys,
I seek to participate in
Life's Olympics
Not as a sprinter
But as a distant runner
To run nonstop in the direction
where I know history awaits me
where true secrets are revealed
where real identities stand out

Each step in the opposite direction
Is a moment of
Enlightenment
Empowerment
Each step back is a step
Forward to the present
To the future
In the muddled spaces where
The present suffocates itself,
I breathe freely, though,
Perhaps feeling welcomed
By history's invitation,
History knows that I stand at the
Door and knock,
No longer its prisoner
When I see the door finally ajar
That signals
That for me there is still a chance
To find my way back there
To learn lessons never taught
When we became apathetic role players
In the crossword puzzle of life

Un Flinching Eyes

Eyes looking at me looking at them,
Who are those people known within my soul,
But unknown to me?
Sad eyes staring,
Guarding secrets that neither of us will tell,
Science invited History to merge,
to become partners in forensics,
history shrugged and
declared itself supreme,
leaving me staring at
faces interested in me,
Eyes across the seas, occasionally glance at the
scenes of the events,
protected crime scenes,
guarded by detectives: MASTERS,
specializing in acts of disappearance,
specialists in the arts of evidence suppression,
Eyes staring at me,
I was seen by them before,
perhaps at that point of NO RETURN,
or last seen running scared from
others unknown to me

Unhappy eyes shedding tears
at the failed union of History and Science
Resulting in my orphanage,
I put out a call to **D N A**,
that laughed uncontrollably
at the thought of fusing with history
in solving the riddle
of the eyes that can't blink,
Faces with eyes fixed on me blush,
I now see my blood highlighted in their veins
in the contours of the facial twists,
signs of the twists of fate

Eyes beckoning me to come closer,
become tools of solid science,
in the most unscientific way,
piercing deep within my soul,
reconstructing histories well-preserved,
mummified within the deepest recess of my identity

Eyes stare at my eyes and my eyes reciprocate,
and invisible signals confirm that
we see the identical prints of the *D N A*,
Eyes that know me intently stare at me
I now know the truth

Disconnection

Appendages,
Attached to banality's ways,
Souls groping in the night
In search of lights designed
To give directions,
Designed to bring
Back on course detached appendages,
Souls aimlessly making their
Way in the most pronounced
Moments of the night,
Incomplete selves
Dependent on rumors of truth,
Rumors of self-reliance,
Of independent appendages
Affixed to life's course
Roving bands of eyewitnesses
Spew out ceaseless venom
Of disclaimers,
Rejecting their own
Complicity in life's Game,
Attachment and detachment
Accomplished in a choreographed
Wild dance of the participants,
Seeking refuge in the bosoms
Of their own lost souls,

Frenzied dances of the implicated
Without pauses
Frenetic dances of the
Fragmented souls
Seemingly trying to detach
Themselves with no success,
Confusion reigns as the appendages
Themselves complicate the
True role of the lost souls,
Appendages now complacent
In their designated state
Move further and further
Away from the ultimate
Integration of the
Constructed self,
An act so brazen
It renders complete chaos

Myafrica

Continent long ago rejected,
Africa thrown from its cradle
--To make room for more *"worthy"* lands,
History rewritten to change the story line,
To change the opening that once read:
Africa, where civilization began,
To now read
Africa, no longer the cradle,
Africa, land of resistance,
Land of my ancestors
Whose blood of defiance mingles
With mine,
Formidable spirits enduring
Daily holocausts,
Humanity not the least bit concerned,
Too busy writing travel tickets for those who sacrificed for me,
Passages fully paid to the new land of freedom,
Full fare,
They called it
THE DARK CONTINENT
And stole innocent lives in the
Opaqueness of the night,
On the continent that still speaks
Volumes of bygone years when
Women
Children
Men
Stood at attention while

Their bodies were
Examined,
Scrutinized
Animalized
Then….
Sold to the highest bidder,
Africa suffered the indignities,
The disgrace
But remained intact,
Strong
Defiant,
Volumes of truth
Seen in its face,
Its hopeful eyes,
Yet in
those blank stares,
Africa endured it all,
and remains
The great
Noble Continent
That it has always
Been,
    Wisdom
    Rebellion
    OPTIMISM

Unspeakable Silence

The earth's core trembled
The seas rumbled
But did nothing to change history's
Sordid course
In the brutal mishandling of Africa's
Most precious gifts,
Converted swiftly,
In record time,
To property, valueless humans
Of great economic value
Status for others,
Africa let go
While the seas and the earth kept vigil
Of history's most heinous
Cowardly act made easy
By a cast of allies salivating for
Flesh sold, bought, resold in the
Bitterness of the silent night
When uninvited visitors came to town
With feign gestures of good will
And a **Sacred Book** clutched securely
under their arms
In the most telling blasphemous
And heretical way

Unbreakale Cycle

Crises emanating from within,
The will to know,
The hope of belonging,
Crises start within, inside
The mind
      Heart
      Soul
Of the one who seeks to recalibrate
The chains of time,
Crises begin within, inside
Inside, within
Linked to a basic need to know
In order to come to terms
With one's own identity,
Complex legacies leave us
Gasping
Sucking air that is branded with the
Word: **L   I   F   E**
But crises are raging,
An ardent fire,
Flames of doubt
Infernos out of control
Igniting more crises within,
Firmly placed inside,
Who is to blame for the
Fire this time
Fires next time
The crises of fire,

Inextinguishable with time?
Crises of identity
Crises of not knowing
And of knowing,
Crises within reek of
Inner turmoil and pain,
Crises of self caused by generations of
--half truths
--half lies
--unfinished narratives
--Silence!

Crises of generations
Creating other generational crises
In a never ending cycle of self-doubt
Alienation, Negation

(Un) Coded

I try to unlock secrets to mysteries
That defy logic,
A daily task,
My voice screams for direction,
Guidance
From those of a higher calling
Who recognize the signal and how
It functions,
I want to be hailed by those
Interpelated to upstage
Life's self-appointed actors
In the final scenes of the drama,
Signals also come to me from afar,
I recognize some,
Question all
For fear of implicating other protagonists
In the remaining acts,
Mysteries, still logical, mystify me,
As I try to demystify them

Caught unguarded in one careless moment,
I clinched my fist, a gesture of defiance
As I inched closer to the secrets of
Decodification,
Stumbling I arrived,
Yet puzzled by the very human spirit
That cajoled me
To open my eyes,
To be witness to
All mysteries,
Even those that have not yet surfaced
And others percolating in spaces
Not so well-defined,
Dreams and mysteries became
entangled,
The process made me opportunistic,
And slowly I began to unlock
The codes
That guard and preserve delicate
And fragile moments

Sworn to secrecy I told the
Voices of the spirits within me
That I would honor the
Protagonists of the mysteries,
And not allow myself to be
Dreamt by the imaginers and inventors
Of history,
I unsealed,
Then unfolded
The parchments that so meticulously
Outline and map the journey that
I must take,
Guided by reliable radars
So accurate that they repositioned me
In the exact spot
That I imagined
Before I myself became protagonized
In those mysteries that lead me
Along converging trails,
To Africa
Long imagined by me
And always a part of my Metalanguage

Voicing Truth

I must find that voice within myself
On the frequency exclusively mine,
          Different voice,
Sound not suitable for the untrained,
Voice not for the NOT ME,
The soul springing ears responds,
Perking ears
Like dogs whining from the
unique frequency waves,
air waves with my markers,
forensics mine!
I really must find
that voice within myself,
to detect the tone that
offsets all other ears
But soothes those belonging to me,
I hear the voice,
only now
am I convinced that
time
     Is
      not
       On
        My
         Side

African Haven

Dungeons with sardonic secrets
Un decoded in the *DNA*
Still recovcrable from invisible
Blood stains,
Each drop narrating a brutal chapter of
Ghana's nightmare,
The screams of unspeakable horrors woke the
Rest of Africa in the middle of the night,
Thinking of you Ghana,
Dungeons guarding in the intricacies of its dusty
Floors stains from
Babies still unnamed,
Future investments for
Those across the Atlantic,
Babies never having seen the sunrise, the sunset
Memorized the darkness with uncanny skill,
The sounds of human tragedy registered
Forever in the tender recesses of their brain
Babies baptized by the UN holy Ghost,
With its creed of greed,
Dungeons with their thick walls,
Their Sacred Wellness Project
To ensure that the
Beasts of burden
Stay long
Stay well

To ensure the economic stability
Across the seas,
Dungeons, big enough to
Stack flesh upon flesh,
Dungeons created by benefactors of
Humankind,
Dungeons of kinship,
Of family reunions,
Dungeons lasting hundreds of years
And telling and retelling stories,
Stories of chains and whips,
Of inverted and diverted dreams
In that majestic castles of horrors,
Dungeons well-equipped for the care
And maintenance of the cargo,
Rotting from lack of care in the
Underbelly of the vessel

Truth Eternal

The boat itself belching, and vomiting blood in a Gory protest,
Unnoticed by the caretakers of the chosen ones,
Dungeons still telling that Ghanaian story,
The African story
That the gate-keepers at the gate of hell
Thought would be stifled,
Forever and ever,
Amen,
Dungeons where whispering voices in the
Counterfeit tranquility of the night recount tales so brutal
They highlight the inadequacies of
Poetic verses,
Yet such tales that need no words
Etched forever in the thick walls
Of the dungeons,
Impenetrable evil
Notarized by spirits,
The unflappable witnesses to the unspeakable
Moments
Linked together by unbreakable seconds of
Wailing voices adjacent to
The GATE of **No Return**,
Where the organizers of the trips
Prepared their manifests
And babies screamed for milk of life,
Bringing sure
Death!

Fragmentation

The world carved in many pieces,
Those making claims for their share
Do so backed by an arsenal of tainted lead
Assured by nuclear expansionism,
The world, carved in many pieces,
Fragmented and disjointed fails to
Reconnect and
Sighs weakly
As its pieces are salvaged
By those whose arsenals of nuclear and unclear technology
Disarm the already dysfunctional GPS of our fate

New Search

Who are we and who do people say we are?
Often conflicting images and interpretation of self
Colliding analyses of identities
Who do we say we are?

We reject random assignments
and opt for our arbitrarily construct of self
Who then are we?
Rejecters of definers of self,
Protest signs clearly denounce the
imposed self-images

Surrounding reflecting mirrors
reveal only what our eyes see in them
and what they choose to see
Or maybe not see

suppressing harsh realties,
challenging our final synopsis
of our lengthy issues of
self

Introspection

Perplexing questions
Leading to no answers,
Yet in the paradox of existence
Having definitive answers
Written somewhere or forever unwritten
In nebulous scripts and scrolls,
Perplexing questions leading somewhere
To our own penchant for understanding ourselves,
Necessary questions imposed by
Nature's firm but undecipherable rules
The human soul resists
Yet seeks responses to the
Most complex inquiries of life,
Perplexing questions leave their
Traits of doubts
Fear
Self-denial
Guilt
And relief from the strangle hold
Of complacency and resignation

Authentication

Irrelevant nations
whose folk do
their ceremonial
signature dance,
movement of
heads, shoulders, waists,
Dance of appeasement,
Compliance dance linked to the
vain attempts at authenticity
recognition
inclusion

No-name nations will their people
to dances of relevancy
to sounds of drums and
pseudo adulation and admiration

Dances reflected in the artistic
motions of the feet,
Judges of the dancers upon the stage
smile sardonically,
An act of approval of the dance,
not of the dancers
dancing with their hearts,
Irrelevant nations performing ceremonies
originating from their souls,
Dancers' souls, impenetrable by
distant observers seeing no
redeeming grace in the choreographed moves of
the insignificant entries cheered on by the
<bequeather> of value points
in the global arena of proposed
human legitimacy

Dream-Like State

Yesterday's dreams,
pseudo realities,
Imitation of life,
dreamers of dreamers of nightmares
hinged to the dreamers' own sense
of a reality created by
dreamers themselves,
two worlds collided
Now juxtaposed and called
ONE,
Imitators intensely dream,
dreading the revealing truth or
lie of their own fragmented reality,
non virtual it may be
Dreamers
Imitators
Illusionists
all perplexed and thwarted by
the sleep-like character
of their true selves

True Humanity

No one knows that you are here
Figment of no one's dreams
no one's brains,
Imagined by few
Dreamt by none,
non-existent in their thoughts
You walk the fields accompanied only
by nature
and occasionally
nature's elements,
non-entity
persona non grata
Dreamers dream dreams of
others not dreaming you,
No one knows your name,
But your deeds are known,
deeds of humanity
the milk of human kindness,
so says Shakespeare
Your imprints leave indelible marks,
imprints of love
of the heart,
Imprints of good will
Proof of your existence,
of you,
dreamt only by you
in your world of reality where
the truth is constantly rebuffed
by rancor and ill will
and an insatiable yearning to
ERASE YOU

Far Away

Distance yourself from the struggle of the poor,
Mutilation of the soul
Numbing of the senses,
Point to them and call them names,
Our societal art
Confront no one,
especially not ourselves
but languish within the banality
of our ways,
reject time's molding technique,
forming
shaping
teaching us to think,
create sufficient distance to snob
our noses,
awful the scent of poverty,
Worse is its potential to shake
us from our apathetic ways,
worse yet the possibility of
less callous hearts
soft souls
self-consciousness

Distance yourself from poverty's sneaky
ways
From the struggle which in mistaken
identity seeks to recruit us
to heights of stellar performances,
Of humanity,
not reflective of
who we really are,
Nor who we wish to be

The Ultimate Game

The wager is on and Greed is set
to win,
No contest,
Win he must,
The bet is on,
Avarice holds the trump card
Deceit backs him
ensuring that the daily itinerary
is followed religiously

Hypocrisy seeks its chance,
no obstacle stands in its way
Facilitating evil's well-carved
Path,
Not true that winners are
predetermined,
Dim light within the dingy room
of wager creates maximum space for
manipulative moves,
shifting hands
sly eyes, trained in the art,
the perverse skill of chicanery

Observe the oldest hand trick
in the book of ideological maneuvers
Victory assured by swift hands
and hardened hearts communicating
openly in ways observers cannot
decode,
The wager is on,
the chief Wager walks away from the
table of treachery
to return later
with improved tricks undetectable by the
human eye and technological accessories
pervading the space of
noble intentions

Por Fin

Pues, me esperabas con paciencia
¡Qué sorpresa que nadie me lo dijera!
Pero todo el mundo sabía que yo vendría
No había secretos en los pueblos
Que algún día te viera yo,
Cuba
Isla de esperanzas y sueños rotos
Una nación con espíritu y ánimo,
Me esperabas,
Cuba,
Para informarme de tu gente
Y de que yo pertenezco acá,
Isleño, caribeño, antillano
Que soy yo,
Esperaste mucho tiempo y me
Saludaste
Pero no te hice caso,
Ahora aquí estoy en
Tu corazón
Viendo a La Habana
Sintiendo a La Habana
Conspirando para ser parte
De ti,
Tan feliz soy, Cuba,
Que me hayas esperado,
Ahora reconozco tu sinceridad
Con tus últimas llamadas
Las llamadas animadas

Que me unieron a ti
De una manera que ni aún tus
Más renombrados filósofos y psicólogos
Pueden explicarlo
(*Translation follows)

===

Finally

So you were waiting patiently for me,
What a surprise that no one told me!
But everyone knew that I would come
No secret in the towns
Not in all the pueblos
That I would someday see you
Cuba
Island of broken dreams and hope
Nation of people with spirit, with zest
You were waiting for me
Cuba

To inform me about your people
To inform me that I belong
Islander, Caribbean man, West Indian
That I am
You waited a long time and waved to me
Along the way
But I did not heed your beckoning
So, Cuba, now here I am in the heart
Of your being
Seeing Havana, feeling Havana
Conspiring to be a part of you,
Cuba, so joyous I am that you waited
And now I know than you were sincere
In your final calls, the spirited calls
That connected me to you
In ways that not even your most
Renowned philosophers and psychologists
Can comprehend!

Esencia Cubana

Traté de construirte en la mente
Oh país de misterio
Y una profunda historia,
De tantos compitiendo por supremacía
Durante la época colonial,
Cuba,
No hay ningún novelista,
No hay artista
Ni sociólogo
Que puedan captar tu
esencia
que puedan asegurar que
entiendan las intersecciones
de tus culturas, tradiciones, y creencias
las contradicciones
las paradojas
la compleja idea de
Raza
africanidad
cubanidad
la esencia isleña
la caribeña,
Me desperté
pensando en cómo
crearte
Pero fracasé

Inundado y abrumado
Por realidades que se intersectan y que
¡Me dejan
jadeante!
(*Translation follows)

===

Cuban Essence

I tried to create you in my mind
Country of mystery
Intense history
Of many vying for supremacy
During the colonial epoch,
Cuba
No novelist, no artist
No sociologist
Can capture your essence
Can claim to understand
The intersections of
Cultures, traditions, beliefs
The contradictions
The paradoxes
The complex idea of
Race

Africanness
Cubanness
Islandness
Caribbeaness,
I awoke devising a plan
          To create you
But failed
Inundated and overwhelmed
By intersecting realities
That leave me
Gasping for air!

Ascendencia

Abuelo se fue y tuvo mucho éxito
Cortando caña y ayudando a sostener
La economía dominicana
Pero también vino acá,
Cuba,
A tus orillas
Para trabajar en los *cañaverales*,
Acá en tu tierra veo rostros
De gente que señala que me conoce
Pues son descendientes de los dedicados cortadores
De caña
Quienes recorrieron nuestras Antillas,
Un día oí una voz,
Examiné uno de los rostros
Lo cual confirmó mi sospecha
(*Translation follows)

===

Ancestry

Grandfather left and excelled at his job
Cutting cane and helping to sustain
La Dominicana economy
But also came here,
Cuba,

To your shores
To work the cane fields, the *cañaverales*,
Here in your land I see faces,
Of people signaling without words that they know me
Because they are descendants of the dedicated cutters
Who traversed our *Antillas*, our West Indies,
One day in la *Habana Vieja*
I heard a voice,
And examined one of the faces,
Confirming my suspicion

Brain Games

To submit your brain to infinite imaginations
Is to invite migraines that know no boundary
How ironic that imagination itself is inadequate,
Powerless
To capture truth from the busy maritime corridors,
Imagination has its place
But discredits my ancestors,
My nameless
Faceless identity-less
Fathers of various fathers and mothers of
Mothers and fathers,
Imagination plays a good game
But shirks its responsibilities
When informed of history's
Long and complex events,
Imagination causes the head to scroll
Filled with blood caused by
Palpitations that result
From the impotency of understanding,
Imagination, you discredit my forbearers,
How nameless they remain!
How faceless they shall always be
But can imagination revive in us
the hope of reconstructing lies?
Reaffirming other truths

Imagination tries to conjure up those moments forever
Uncaptured, lost
At this juncture it is my only
Ally
As I probe deeply into my subconscious
In hopes of re instituting the lives of
Those lost
By a system in complicity with
The sprawling oceans of the world

Right Frequency

Voices that once soothed
Now utter a sound unknown
to the heart,
Echoes emanating from the sound
represent vain repetitious acts,
acknowledged by none
in the soul's sphere,
Now only screams are heard
disingenuously masquerading
as the original voices of reason
that extended beyond the periphery

The heart's main borders only manage
faint whispers of disclaimers,
no longer seeing itself in the
pivotal role,
Voices that once enchanted
like the snake charmer,
orchestra leader of his band of vipers,
Now hoarse from their misrepresentations,
fake replicas of voices,
that calm roaming spirits tuned in
to the frequency of sounds,
only tangentially known to
those characters who in the
past vociferously boasted of
life altering sounds that
they knew so well

Nación Unica

País complicado
Nación compleja
Mi isla vecina, esta Cuba
En Holguín, Matanzas, La Habana Vieja
Se ven varias imágenes
De esta región caribeña
Patria de Lima, Morejón
Pedroso, Guillén
Dentro de ella diversidad cultural sin fin
Una bella física, pero aún más del alma
Llegué a sus orillas tratando de entenderla
Con la meta de acercarme más a mi isla hermana
(*Translation follows)

===

Unique Nation

Complicated country
Complex nation
My neighboring island, this Cuba
In Holguín, Matanzas, La Habana Vieja
Various images of this Caribbean nation
Lima's, Morejón, and Guillén's

Country
Cultural diversity without end
A physical beauty, but more so of the soul
I came to her shores trying to understand her
With the goal of getting closer to my sister island

Cubafrica

Qusiera definirte,
Cuba, si me lo permitieras,
Eres el Continente en América
Transformada por el proceso
De <transculturación>
Pero andando en América
Bien vestida del gran Continente,
Te pido una oportunidad de
Categorizarte, nación antillana,
Con la promesa de hacerlo
Con pocas palabras,
O con una sola,
Decir que eres tú,
Sin duda,
Cuba,
<Africa>

===

Cubafrica

I would like to define you,
Cuba, if you would allow me,
You are the Continent in Latin America
Transformed through the process
Of <transculturation>

60

But walking in Latin America
Dressed up in Africaness
I beg you for the opportunity
To categorize you, West Indian nation,
With the promise that I will do so
in a few words,
or in one word only,
And say that you are
Undoubtedly,
Cuba,
<Africa>

Reflexión

Escribir sobre ti, Cuba,
Es imaginarte en tu larga historia,
Ecos de gritos de seres humanos
Transportados a tus orillas
Sin ninguna consideración
Por las almas destruidas en un avalanche
De decisiones amargas,
Ambiciones codiciosas, avariciosas,
Ver tu tierra expansiva
Es ceder a emociones multiples
Sobre la opresión en siglos pasados
Sobre la explotación y subjugación
Por los poderosos en aquel entonces,
Versificar sobre ti, isla contradictoria,
Es sentir el espíritu
De un alma que se ha despertado
Viéndose a sí misma en un
Reflejo de los rayos de esperanza
Producidos por un brilliante
Sol antillano
(*Translation follows)

===

62

Reflection

To write about you, Cuba
Is to imagine you in your long history
Echoes of screaming beings
Transported to your shores,
Without any consideration
For the souls destroyed in an avalanche
Of bitter decisions,
Greedy and avaricious ambitions,
Seeing your expansive land
Is to yield to multiple emotions
About oppression in past centuries
About exploitation and subjugation
By the powerful during that time,
To create verses about you, contradictory island,
Is to feel the spirit
Of a soul that has now awaken
Seeing itself in the reflection
Of the rays of hope,
Produced by a brilliant West Indies sun

PART II

Tic-Tock

Time's throbbing motion to awake,
to disturb sleepwalkers strolling idly by,
boisterous sounds of
seconds
minutes
hours
the tick-tock of the worn out clock
nailed to the wall
crucified unjustifiably,
But still serving
as major recorder of missed opportunities,
lost by the sleepwalkers of time,
restless souls moving in circles,
see nothing
Ears not hearing the deafening sounds of
time
ignore its guiding principles and
misinterpret the intent of the
cacophonic clock

The coma-like state of the dreamers
precludes a heightened level of consciousness
of existence, of urgency
The tic-tock sound of the clock
lulls the walkers to ultimate levels of
the subconscious
But fails to awake them from their
deep sleep,
all asphyxiated by apathy's deadly
choke hold
In a far reaching globalization of indifference

Protect The Land

Do it in the name of homeland
Create enemies,
enemies of the state
Defy, denigrate
while earning compliance
through might,
testosterone power,
and
economic arm wrestling,
combat your enemy combatants
and make them cry
U-N-C-L-E and bow in reverence
as they see within the schema
essence of your Goodness
Mercy
Morality
Ethics
emanating from your gentle spirit
All tied to the mandate sent from
above,
manna from heaven

Angel manna
Prophet manna
manna of the deity
war manna to
quell wars
Homeland security manna
bountiful manna of abundance
stifling the combatants, the enemy combatants
sent by Lucifer and his rebellious band
of misfits,
To ensure homeland security
suspend freedom
Do it in the name of the homeland

Invoke new laws, reinterpret others
Silence countries spying you spying them
Silence all, then follow their trails,
Learn their profiles in the secretive
outmoded index cards of the Library of Congress
And in acrobatic surfs of the Internet Highway

Place Of Love

Complex world
technological infusion,
Intersection with that other world
Concocted, and constructed also,
Building blocks of concrete insensitivity,
The world,
Call it yours
and set it on its head,
YOURS,
Privilege of ownership
entitlement
stringed in hierarchal order,
those deemed yours
--lower
--less
--inferior
Border, or non border countries
States within,
Katrina remembered!
Come to the table and drink from the
common cup of spoiled milk of
inhumane kindness

Complex new world order,
Inverted world
in which communion takes
place in inversion
within the reach of those
whose heads are the foot rest
for those who love their
neighbors
as they love themselves

Trusted Friend

Judas approached, I barely smiled
His sweaty palms told tales undeniable
by either him or me,
things I could not comprehend,
and then echoes of
promises
adulation,
He crowned me king of kings
then placed a throng around my head,
admiration
recognition
He claimed me Lord of Lords!
In a game of blasphemy and heresy

Judas approached me,
He knew me well and smiled
This time a hearty one,
when I could not,
and he laughed
and watched through the corner
of his eyes
As in vain I tried again
to smile
to laugh,
Judas called me
I knew his last name and
repeated it to myself,
I recognized his voice of enchantment,
Even before he murmured
    "30 PIECES OF SILVER"
No kiss on the cheek was necessary,
The whisper told the tale,
A tale that only the inimitable Judas
could tell

All Ours

Owners of land, in our own names
Provinces in principalities
Ownership, the ultimate bragging
rights
Mines, not yours,
Ours, not theirs,
Earth, Seas with our names
etched in them
Ocean waves spelling our name
with each ebb and flow

Earth proudly announcing
it belongs to us,
Owners of places, of palaces,
and of land
of mountains
and mountain ranges
of peaks and valleys,
The land is mine
My name embedded in the
earth's core,
My houses, extensions of myself,
Owner of houses and things
Owner of things and People
Owners of People and things,
People cargo
Cargo people

I follow a rich tradition that makes
me complacent and content
knowing that my worth
my goodness
my value is inseparable from
my possessions
thus I bask in the sun
and from time to time make
sure that my name is irrevocably
inscribed on the rocks and stones
even in the underbelly of the
earth's core.
Yes!

Return Policy

Earth is reclaiming its own,
the prophets speak in language,
that we,
in arrogance shun,
and laugh at,
a sardonic laughter that
incriminates us,
as victims of
our own conceit,
carved into unrecognizable
pieces by the sharp edges
formed by the intersection of
who we are
and who others construct us to be.

Nature is reclaiming its own,
amidst our eyes, and
helpless arms, unable to
reach,
unable to negotiate with
her agents--
hurricanes
cyclones
tsunamis,
typhoons
earthquakes,
all ruffling the earth's core,
while cacophonic noises from the gales
speak in scripted language
the prophets' truths,
that the earth is reclaiming its own,

snow drifts,
rock hard ices storms,
storming the nights,
too cold and lethargic
the night wanderers
mumble in silence
something about prophets and
the reclaiming of nature's
designated territories

Hat Of Tricks

Tricks of the head deceive us,
unplanned strategies
slippery stuff, sleight of hand,
centuries of successful tricks
–war tricks
oppression tricks
discrimination tricks
ideological tricks
and traps,
planned strategies,
tricks designed never to fail
–economic suppression tricks
–expansionist tricks
–global usurpation tricks
–new immigration policies tricks,
dwarfing the Anti Terrorist Act
of 1996
Patriot Act tricks
Election tricks
Tricks of Life
Tricks of Death

Nations, world, like a meteor
pulled swiftly downward by gravity
willfully forceful ways,
Tricks of the head and hand
the mind
the soul
Tricks of the heart
Tricks to ensure that all tricks
are maintained intact,
the art of the trickster,
the inner workings
of the magician of fate of others,
Tricks of the head deceive us all
and leave barely enough
room for recovery

Life and Death now paired together as
one in the ultimate trick of time

Power Of Illusions

Brightness dimmed by nature's chief nemesis,
Insensitivity!
Concocted images
Flickering, ostentatious lights
Showing evidence of strain,
Lights offset by devious acts
Then rendered authentic by design
Yet undetected by the designers themselves
Of the crafty arts within the acts of representation,
Misrepresentations and
Re presentations that stand in as proxy
As throngs of beings resign themselves
To their fate,
Locked into cells of illusions,
Complacent all,
Nightmarish dreams of yesteryear
Dreams of darkening firmaments and skies,
Of nebulous silhouettes marking time of life,
Obscurity renames itself THE FUTURE,
Feigning alliance with fate's allies,
All on cue to succumb to illusion's most
Salient art—
Its unbridled penchant to deceive

Shall The First Be Last?

The *first President* that looked
differently
Endured years of suspicion,
Denial of birthright
Linked to various religious institutions
Cast as racist, elitist, hateful, aloof,
Inhumane,
Responsible for international chaos,
The world's ills,
For the attacks in Paris,
Brussels,
The reason USA did not win gold in
The 100 meters,
Yes, Creator of Ebola!
That *first President* who looked nothing
Like The **First President**!

Market rises, success denied!
Unemployment plummets
Credit neglected!
Peace at home
Acknowledgement delayed!
Health Plan installed,
Read as death squad handbook!
The *first President* that
Looked like me cried "*foul*"
And was met by jeers and stares
And
HATE
And disrespect for the sacred
Institution,
Arm bearing men reciting
Their second amendment rights
Casually occupying spaces
Historically reserved for
The Leader of the land,

The *first Prez* became the first President
Denied the legitimacy of the presidency,
In a paradoxical entanglement- -
Deemed fit to win an election but unfit-
For occupancy in the White House,
Not a place for the *first President* who looked not
Like the **First President,**
nor any of the previous ones
nor the successive president,
LOSER OF THE POPULAR VOTES!
The *first President* given his papers
To return to majestic Kenya
Great land of the Continent,
Of the world,
His mythical birthplace,
Yet real,
Fictionalized by multiple
Conspiratorial plans, maybe
Not written but concocted by spirits
Of evil
Proud Kenya, the great ancestral home
Opened its arms and beckoned
The *first President*
"Come my child!"

Kenya, and all of Africa poised
To counteract the evil spirits
Lurking in the deepest enclaves of
Human hearts

The *first President of the US*
That look differently
Vaguely guarded by
The Secret Service smiled
And was rewarded by vitriolic frowns
From those regretting the experiment,
By those voting to prove
The prognosticators wrong:
That a land seeking to right itself
From unspeakable acts
Could put in the White House
The *first President* and his
Presidential family looking nothing
Like the **First President**
Who by his skin hue
Set the rules for Presidential authenticity

Story Retold

Revisionists write in their LAST WILL AND TESTAMENTS
"Slavery was an aberration"
The purifiers of history's sordid narratives
Give their final words on a deathbed of roses
"The enslaved would have been enslavers if granted the opportunity"

History's interpreters exclaim: *"We do not see the scars from the system,"*
The anointed literary gatekeepers fictionalize accounts
"The numbers are too exaggerated,"
The guardians and the guards of
TRUTH
Are more blunt:
"Slavery is a figment of the collective imagination"

And spirits already restless
Shake even more as the echoes from
These voices rattle them at the core,
And they refuse to be silent,
Spirits of my ancestors challenge the
Detractors
The re-writers,
The new hermeneutics
the new truths
the fiction of "*the fiction of slavery,*"
Spirits always looming near
refuse to smile
and we see in their fixed gazes
the same rebellious eyes that
characterized them before,
the same eyes that debunked the
myth of
docility
surrender
passivity
resignation

Fumes come from the mouths of the spirits
And ashes crumble non-stop,
From their eyes spring tears of fire,
The spirits have heard the voices of
History's new writers,
Of history's new storytellers
The spirits of our ancestors screamed:
"I must speak!"
The spirits of those held to be undone
Can only *speak truth*

And what better witnesses,
Cuddled in the pitch of the dark
Recording every sight,
Every sound,
Every emotion!
The spirits did their job to perfection
All revisionists,
detractors,
pseudo interpreters
Fairytalers!
Inventors and benders of truth--
SILENCE!

Joie De Vivre

Echoing sounds
Emanating from the valley
Where separated souls chat and sing
Sing and chat
In praise of yet another day
Of communion with family
Communication with friends
Noisy sounds of joy
As humanity sneers at fate's secrets weapons
Reserved for moments of envy,
Weapons aimed at those daring
To value life,
Camaraderie,
Friendship,
Fate, surnamed Destiny,
Frowns as the reverberating sounds of joy
Joie de vivre
Fill the valley's darkness
And streams of contentment
Gush forth,
Inundating the centers of professed gloom,
Debunking the myths of eternal sufferings
In earth's endless valleys of prescribed doom

The Witnesses

The earth's core trembled
Upon sensing the human violations
Occurring above ground,
Tremors moved in the deepest
Recesses of the ocean vast
Made aware of the subjects
Carried by the torrents just above
The heart of the complicit oceans
Claiming ignorance in an historic
Transportation scheme
Linking nations of all continents
In a diabolic contract of convenience,
The seas and the earth knew the truth
As it reverberated in their underbellies,
They trembled and shook
But committed themselves to fulfilling
Their joint mission as co conspirators
In the elaborate plan for profit
Emanating from cold, bloodless veins,
The land, the seas, the skies
All knew, because all bore witness
To the horrors—
--Dehumanization
--Desecration of humanity,
--Larceny of innocence of children
--Never reaching adulthood,
--Dreams curtailed forever

While the earth and the seas trembled
In a game of pretense,
In the calmness of the night,
The bidders offered their bids
For merchandise coming out
Of the womb of the formidable Continent
That did not smile, nor grin
As arms of lead and steel
Silenced the will of resistance,
So Africa gave up her children
In a blaze of heat and fire,
Generating from the flames,
Emanating from the guns,
The carbine rifles
With Signature:
"Contract for life and human destruction"

Endless Quest

I looked deep within whom I thought I was,
Constant echoes of myself reverberating
against walls difficult to negotiate

I searched well within me,
within whom I said I was
and saw vibrating cells suggesting
LIFE,
Probing deeper finally I detected me,
The *<me>* I was desperately trying to
define

"Try a trick," I urged,
so clearing my eyes
I envisioned me,
clearly set apart from the *"self"*
constructed without consultation with the *<I>*
and the *<me>*,
I sensed the subtle integration of the two,
yet so far apart

Looking once more surmised I
"Who I am can no longer dislodge itself
from who I want to be
and who I thought myself to be,"
I looked even deeper into myself and
was struck by the
clarity of my epiphany:
The gradual comprehension of my singular role within the
Well-*un*defined parameters of the
politics of self

Fortification

Inner strength forged from
Within seemingly surrendered souls
Not at all bewildered by the battles
Waging outside,
Finding none of this daunting,
Inner strength propelled then sustained
By that singular factor—knowledge of self
Appreciation of self,
Inner strength emanating from a fortress
Well-entrenched within the multiple
Definitions of who we are
Inner strength asserting,
Affirming its presence
Underwhelmed by the infinite signifiers,
Inner strength, our virtue,
Standing the test of time
Stabilizing the ozone with its layers
Of purified air,
Polluted zone often so envious
Seeking to destabilize all
in its quest to claim victory
over our beings,
The effort will fall short
Because strength is nurtured
Forever by eternal springs
Situated securely within the core of
Our authentic selves!

Inverted Freedom

(For Ruby Simmonds)

The notion of freed slaves is paradoxical,
A kind of oxymoronic interplay
But nothing at all contradictory about
Battered ships
Shackled wrists and ankles,
Shackled souls!
Is history too long,
its moments distended
like a stomach suffering from mal nutrition?

Hide the deeds of the protagonists' history,
under bloated moments, symptomatic of a lack of care,
Filter all moments through a sieve of trickery
which in its complex array of skills
inverts the moments of truth in
a larger scheme of
Distortions

Invert also the protagonists' roles
in the
shadowy silhouette of the moments,
their newly constructed roles
made permanent by time's dizzying
spells

The sub-characters,
the interpreters of history,
stop in their tracks, speechless,
with no clear sense of
unraveling the mystery of the
bloated moments
and thus with no method of
deciphering the paradoxical formula
of the FREED Slave
antithetically paradigmatic structure

Journey Of The Mind

High above,
clouds visibly angry with
the constellation burning through
them mercilessly,
Clouds of multiple formations,
lead me on journeys of imagination
Clouds of centaurs
of half-man, half-beast,
Clouds refusing to smile,
mouth closed, filled with
water still performing the chores
of the day
Bull clouds
Clouds of mansions
Romantic clouds
Clouds of chariots
Monster clouds
Majestic clouds of sweet dreams
above the firmaments,
Lazy clouds reposed on
bays and sand-cloaked beaches,
waiting impatiently for dawn,
Clouds peeking from above
look at me with scorn,
I can only surmise
disappointed at me for using them
for imaginative flights of fancy

Non Instructions

No signs clearly written to instruct travelers
Who once they choose their paths
will sit
Complacent
Heaping praise upon themselves for a job
Well done!
No signs to confirm
the journey's designated track

No signs of signs
to instruct which way to go,
yet, signs of life!
No signs of signs,
Open space,
No real truths
And no signs that signify that
singular truth- -
of no signs

Open space, insecurely set
Between wider spaces
Where no signs are seen
And thus,
No bearers of the signs
that outline the path that
travelers should choose

Permutations

Years pass revealing little or nothing
Of the rules to follow,
Or how not to live,
But giving unfinished models
Of how to pursue this journey,
We take no time to reflect,
To ponder the greatest mystery
Of all
The mystery of the existence of
Humankind
The many permutations, endless in fact,
Infinite combinations of life's possibilities
Impossible to control,
Infinity runs wild throughout
The corridors of life
And there is not yet a heroine,
Or hero,
To corral the ever reformulating
Strings of realities
In a largely incomprehensible act
Of life's various machinations

Trick Mirrors

Images of distorted images of ourselves
Counterfeit outlines of who we are
Brought about by the signals sent
By minds subjected to
Prominent vices

Images in mirrors that reflect
Already twisted reflections,
Self-images are true but
Truth is now fluid
Truth cannot truly be defined,
Thus
Images of distorted images of who we are

Counterfeit souls,
No way to authenticate all the symbols
On the bill itself,
As we step before the mirror,
Truth-- The king of distortion--in its
Own sheepish way,
Admits (a rare occurrence) its legacies of
Lies,
Images, false and twisted, are
Truth's claims to our
   REAL
   Selves

Independence

Extended branches well beyond
their prescribed range
Providing shade to shield
from Ray,
the sun's boy
Waiting its turn,
Overarching branches
create new spaces
open spaces
free spaces,
courtesy of their
desire for independence,
Well-extended branches living
their own lives
existing within
spaces,
vacuum of spaces,
link vacant dreams set in
a nightmarish mode,
Branches seeking their own
Way,
Oblivion their aim,
Moving branches
shaking branches
upset by the daily wind spasms,
Hoping to upend the seemingly
endless extensions

The Fire Within

Subtle quest for freedom,
burning from within
raging, uncontrollable flames,
ruled by the arson squad probing its cause
"wild fire not deliberately set"

Society of performance of the
exterior art of imagery
and images contradict the official cause of
the fire: *<Fire purposely set,*
ARSON>

Society, master of the external,
condemns the perceived arsonists
for creating chaos when none
was necessary,
Fire within rages and the
infernal light sends signals that
freedom's quest has very little to
do with the analysis of
the raging flames

Un Liberated

Prisons with no walls,
Made not of steel
nor brass,
Captivating space suppressing will,
Incarceration with no known bars,
Long-term sentences
in the iron--less cell of nature's handiwork
ostentatiously displayed within the
quiet space
with no walls
with no brass
no chains
no iron links
Solitary confinement
Lone self,
by proxy,
Self by default
No bars
No cells
No chains
No walls
Life sentences in
Bar-less
Cell-less
Wall-less prisons
are pronounced endlessly under the
watchful sentinels of the
MIND

The Last Will Without Testament

Self-appointed guardians of the world,
Nations of unlimited power in collusion
plan their clandestine meetings
to regulate
to orchestrate,
leaders par excellence of weaker
gentler nations,
Patriarchy gone bad,
Bands of seekers of order,
seekers of realignment
world order assignments
Called to arms by themselves,
self-appointed
self-anointed
executors of the Will of the
estate of food-seeking nations
poverty driven countries
disease ravished lands

executors of the estate
executioners of the
will of people,
exacting blood
of
unlimited quantity

Celestial Encounter

angels at the doors that don't open
blow celestial horns,
resonating echoes create awkward
waves of sea-like clouds
held in check by an unassuming sky
and vague memories of
nature's initial plans

archangels soar with radar-like
precision and explore from afar the closed
doors and
the <terre firme> corrupted
by its inhabitants,
by time
struggling to juggle minutes irrevocably lost

gale storms winds
and global shifts
formed from the vibrating doors
trying to be pried open by
wingless enemies of the angels
and archangels,
Cherubim and Seraphim

sounds of trumpets
instrumentation of the science of life,
still evident behind doors that
will not open,
band of angels
hosts of archangels with their
supporting casts summon strength
tied to life's signals

behind the closed doors,
melodious sounds, sounds of harmony
harmonious sounds of melody
Music of the orchestra of life,
expert musicians serenading the
"*terra firme*"
from their position adjacent to the
closed doors
constantly cognizant of the narrative silently
being scripted behind the doors,

the narrative
long established,
now embedded in the unparallel
melody of the unheralded musicians
making music sanctioned by the angels
patiently waiting at the
unopened doors that
oxidize
and asphyxiate with time

Garden Of Eden

Pacifiers of history
Discounting pages,
diaries of bitter truth,
squirming uneasily,
startling realities breed disquieted
spirits,
History's primary mythicists in constant
Denial,
Doctors attending to history's
deep open wounds of excessive time,
Diagnosis: < *historical psychosis,*
provoked by failing memory>
Prescription: <*softeners of hard facts, one tablet*
as needed>
Romanticizers of life's real experiences
seeking flowers in the rose garden of
historical illusions:
Condition detected: <*hallucinatory, delusional,*
in need of analysis>,
Rose Garden walkers,
Flowers blooming, glittering in the sun,
Weeds unnoticed,
Olive branches growing
in the Garden of make believe,

Branches now extended,
broken branches
broken in the long process of the
transformation of historical moments
into mythical fabrications

Reconfiguration

No echoes,
No shadows,
only resonating imitations of the sounds
Emanating from the earth's core,
the center piece of nature's silent narrative,
The earth, supposed designated omniscient narrator,
Reads from its preliminary drafts
of nature's script
while timid observers of the processing of life
Agree to withhold judgment

Taking the cue, the reliable
narrator recounts life's moments
and in this enunciation of
the chronology
There are outlines of shadows,
There are sounds
and echoes
that clearly resonate,
shaking the core,
The center of life's
Master Narrative

The Spies

The leaves on that tree seem
not to know who I am,
Nor do they seem to care
Yet in some fashion their movements want

To confirm a suspicion that we are connected
By life's rules to each other,
The leaves on that tree that don't care to know me
Blow in the wind, the same wind that calms my spirit

And there is a heightened sense of a note of
Disassociation sent by the tree and its leaves

The branches of the tree with the leaves that demonstrate
No tender moments, no proof of their own sense of belonging,
Speak no words of wisdom to me, but stand still
As I negotiate my way through the same thicket where they stand

I sense that they are spying me as I twist and turn
Wounded by the very motions that define who I am,
They see me, but speak no words, no words of wisdom,
As I do the dance that they themselves cannot do

But it is a dance akin to the movements of the leaves
Resulting from the action of the wind, the same wind
That calms this spirit.
The leaves on that tree do not know who I am
And care not

I can only look as the branches
And the tree itself protest in
Silence,
An act so vain that the winds
Blowing forcefully before
Now cease,
In a pronounced moment of recognition
Of endless paradoxes

Winding Road

Why try to unravel this *long* journey,
at times so *short*,
journey of short strides that cover
a long undetermined distance,
journey that does not announce its
itinerary,
agenda-less trip,
series of coincidences, arbitrariness,
or planned occasions?

At its last meeting nature's agents
spoke freely of the contradictions
and conflicts along the long journey,
with no clear signs of the end,
yet the end comes with its sure
markers of time,
the principal agent,
familiar with every segment of the
trip

Many who tried to unravel it all
say
"to no avail"
for this journey follows its
own fixed rules
within the series of coincidences
and arbitrariness
not yet
agreed upon by the
weary travelers
seeking shelter
and refuge in this time ravished
space

Unsealed Record

Chronicles of life's journey,
fast paced trip
signs ignored or
misunderstood
unheralded journey, lost time
leading to no place,
all places,
The trip to nowhere,
non exotic trip to somewhere

Chronicles of life's journey vaguely recorded,
within me records of strife,
of gains,
losses,
Challenges met and surpassed,
hope stifled by anti-agents
antagonists of self
Chronicles of life,
no time to answer the question
burning within me- -
What do these
chronicles
really say
about me?

Second Chance

On life's second voyage we will embark
To search for secrets, secrets of friendship
And unlock the formulas
of hate
of generosity
of avarice
of loyalty
of treachery
But only on life's other voyage that
promises pristine waters
unadulterated air
non suffocating space,
The lion and the lamb together
as stated in the Word,
When the second journey is complete
there will be rejoicing as the
voyagers find, then decipher all
riddles,
Riddles all finally decoded,
on the second voyage
With voyagers set
to understand the evidence
left by life's FIRST voyager,
like Columbus' cryptic code
and detailed summaries

Oilinone

Snake oil
manufacturer boasting of his product's
high quality
limitless quantity,
Bargain sale,
snake oiler traversing the land,
the land of others
proud of his wares,
oil that heals,
charming oil,
oil of life
Of the soul

Snake artist at his craft,
dexterity, undeniable trait
of this producer of serpent oil,
top of the line,
all purpose transformative oil,
top feature: universality, globality
flawless, colorless, odorless
lubricant oil
emanating from the snake,
the property of the
owner,
the vendor of transforming arts

Sign seen in the distance:
OIL FOR SALE
BARGAIN DEAL,
Snake oiler pushing his wares
Pushing out the pushers,
the narco kings,
slippery oil coming non stop,
product of the oil viper
beaming
rejoicing
celebrating
his chief product
leaving its lasting imprint on
society's impressionable soil

GENTLE BREEZE OF un HUMAN KIND ness

Battles initiated by the wind's
Violent breezes blowing humanity in
Collision courses,
Wild wind uprooting emotions of
Human frailties,
International sparring matches,
Clashes caused by the wind of HUMANKIND
Clashes of
Greed
Bitterness
Evil,
Oh untamed wind blowing
Antagonists in the same direction
Bringing them together,
Clashing heads!
Winds initiating battles so fierce,
So intense in an awkward ceremony
of paralysis and abandonment,
Fierce winds of time
Created not by nature
But by the forces of humanity
In a frantic search for itself,
Guaranteeing **W**aves of
Mass **D**estruction

The Quiet Street

Wall Street sang its own praise:
The capitalist system is flawless,
Money will flow infinitum from all
Modes of production
The Street saw its work and declared:
All is well!
The Street molded itself,
Then other nations in its own image
Of unabashed capitalism

Wall Street promised unlimited income,
And retirements for disciples of
the Gospel of Capitalism,
Disciples and apostles all
We genuflected and in so doing
Willed our capital
To those on the Street with the tag
We guarantee your financial future,
Wall Street looked at its missionary work,
And claimed: *"It is the true will of God!!"*

Wall Street had answers for
Weakening stocks
Fading bonds
Uncertain Futures,
The Street boasted:
"We are the Masters of the Capital,"
But had no answer for
Greed
Avarice
Selfishness
Arrogance
Self-interests
Lack of ethics,
Just as these vices began to take hold
Wall Street closed its eyes,
The Street kept silent,
mum,
while the promoters of Evil vices
Disrupted ideal notions of Capitalism
And restructured the Street
Forever and ever
AMEN

The Dwelling Place

Who besides Hitler and his unlimited gang of henchmen
will dwell in the lake,
the lake of fire and brimstones
attracting like a magnet venomous characters,
maggots of humanity,
anti-heroes?

Contemporary society thrives on its short time memory,
history purged by amnesia,
self-delusion,
revision,
history buried under the weight
of lies
distortions
pretensions

Who then will dwell with Adolph?
history merged with virtual reality
becoming real by default
by proxy,
only Hitler?
Or will he be joined by the architects of slavery's
anarchical structure, eternal separation, damnation

Just Hitler?
Or will he be accompanied
by the overseers and the whip slingers,
the slave owners and
benefactors of the institution,
enforcers and traffickers of the trade?
The designers of the holes of hell
in the well-constructed ships and schooners
that guaranteed first class transportation of
the human cargo of degradation,
dehumanization?

The designers forgot
To assign themselves beds
Adjacent to Adolph,
Will the mastermind be yoked with the chief whip man?
The lynchers, who partied at their ceremonies?
Lynching Inc,
Good Business,
play the castration numbers game,
dismemberment,
One-foot slave cannot flee,
no foot slave can't escape,

Bounty hunters of slaves
encouraged and supported
by the Congress of the land,
sanctioned by federal laws,
civilians deputized on the spot
complicity in the capture game,
the game of prey
No-hand slave **must not** STEAL food,
such acts of immorality
such lack of ethics,
on the part of the slave

Teach them well,
to obey
to respect
to appreciate
their privileged status
hierarchical arrangement,
house slaves will prosper

but who then will be with Hitler?
will the revered and the heralded,
leaders of the strongest nations in the world
on their thrones of illusion of goodness?
better not to defile their sacred place in history's
mythical structure already secured

Is there a special place for
owners of slaves who participated in the
great genocide project, still barely recorded,
so fresh in history still?
No!
Those were just the times we say,
so then, only Hitler shall dwell in his
amply spacious house of doom,
YES! Hitler all alone!

At Last WMD

Searching for weapons
designed to curtail humanity
they found none,
thus the new war
formerly predicated on fear of
projected extinction of the WESTERN WORLD,
was postponed,
long enough to change goals:
regime change
urgency here
more imminent
more noble
more appropriate
No *WMD* but the leaders
of good in the paradigm
GOOD VERSUS EVIL
surge on

Westernize the rest,
uncivilized nations, in need of
cultural appropriations
No *WMD*
but that matters not,
bring them to the fold,
to the center of CULTURE
the place where higher forces
are designated as the core of
truth
No *WMD*?
Maybe of **M**ass **D**eception?
But truth reigns and
guards against other unspoken
but proven acts of domination

Toys Not For Boys

War of words,
Not of conscience,
Tongue skirmishes,
loose tongues spewing ideology unfit for
human consumption,
Awkward moments forced out to the
periphery of time,
Conflicts of the soul,
and over the Soil,
Conflicts raging over the spoils,
Staged demonstration performed in the
Theater of the absurd
Arsenal of toys,
For the impatient boys,
Contingency measures to support
Play War
Play Guns
Play injuries
in the well-staged bellicose art
for the entertainment of viewers,
Directors of the stellar performances
bask in the flow of limitless
accessibility to the
Play Station,
Game Boy never unplugged!

Boys of the summer,
of winter and spring
masters of their toys,
cache of weaponry
Toys of fun
Noisy toys
Silent toys
Toys with no smiley faces
War of words
Words of war
Battles not of the mind
openly set in the vast arena
with ample space,
space toys activity,
Toys eternally plugged into
real monitors capturing each moment
of contusions and disfigurement

Freedom Request

Where is our conscience,
while grains are served and we sit
detached at the table
chewing to oblivion
our daily bread?
Send the crumbs to half-naked continents,
"**_FEED THE POOR_**"
a motto with no ring,
no meaning to us,

Be free conscience,
free from the
story that you know well,
free yourself from weighty, bulky evidence of
plight
free thyself, conscience, and allow the being
beaming within you to sup
in good faith at the table of flesh
while semi-naked nations fret too much
because of slow moving meals and grains

Dwell in peace, conscience,
chew with reckless abandon
the meat fit for kings and queens of
conscience-less caring nations,
Conscience, really, free thyself!

The Head Of Normalcy

Cat scan of the brain: *"NORMAL"*
Actions defy the latest read,
Rebel acts,
Acts of Domination,
Brain waves read: *no irregularity,*
MRI confirming the scan's analysis,
incomprehensible human behavior,
Nations trampled,
They shiver reading the warning signs:
*"Consequences for not following the
orders of compliance"*

Scans do not lie,
just segments of truth they tell
Normal waves of brain,
No explanation for roving
bands of pirates with
No abnormality
No aberration,
No explication
for activities not predicted
by the SCAN OF THE HEAD
on the shoulders erect,
beaming with pride
to host a head of that caliber

Stealth For Good Health

Bombers silenced disobedient nations
People defying alliance
Self-preservation
Pinpoint accuracy
collateral damage
generations of idealism curtailed,
of youth seeking their place
in a world bent on
erasing them,
global eradication,
Honorable Stealth,
humble nation, yet arrogant
enough to reject servitude
enslavement
subjugation
Stealth, extension of hormonal secretion
tied to the most innate savage nature
of MASCULINITY,
Rivals fall to their knees
subconsciously genuflecting to
The WMD bounty hunters,
themselves committed to the
legacy of the honored Stealth

The Secret Club

(For Avani Z. White, Ahsir Z. White, Amari Z. White, Asha Z. White, and I. Sekou White)

You smiled at me,
Though many said "*babies don't smile*"
But you did smile at me
I knew why
But everyone else was guessing,
You smiled,
Like your brother had done
Years before, sending signals of
    Belonging
    Connection
    Recognition
    Love
We spoke only through smiles
That first day,
You knew who I was,
That I would call you AVI,
But kept that knowledge secretive
While others falsely attribute your smiles
To a natural baby twitch,
Stomach gas,
But you smiled at me
Because you knew the truth
That your brother also knew,

The truth that
You are the princess,
Your brothers the princes of a grandmother
You know and will always know
Through the vividness of the
Imaginary
Rooted in the reality of her goodness,
You will always know her
And will smile in a way that only
She
I
And YOU
Will fully comprehend

You Belong To Her

**(For Ahsir Z. White, Avani Z. White, Amari Z. White,
Asha Z. White, I. Sekou White)**

Ahsir, the little heavyweight
Weighing in with style
Your undeniable presence,
Waiting for you
Your brother
Your big sister
She who prefers to define you
As Baby Brother
Here you are my little one,
Loved by all
And guarded and smiled upon
By a grandmother who has
Not seen you
But, smiled the same way
She did when your siblings made their entry,
Now here you are
Happy, at peace,
Knowing that
Your grandmother would
Take one look and say:
"Yes you are mine!"
You took your time
And enjoyed the journey
To the new world,

Your face clear evidence
Of a joyous past,
Connected to one who
Nurtured your way here
In the flashing lights
Of the new world
Its noise,
Its hustle and bustle
But you endured it all with a shrug
Like your brother and sister
Did before,
Setting a shining example for
Little big brother,
Happily making his presence
Known on the 6 day of November
2015----------
9:26 am

===

My Original Inner Truths

--A lead singer may have the voice of a nightingale, converted to that of an owl without his/her backup chorus
--Acknowledge those who touch your hand, cherish those who touch your heart

--Allow no one to define the parameters of your success through concocted notions of who you are or should be
--Arrogance inevitably breeds complacency, itself a blueprint for failure
--Audacity may at times disguise itself as assertiveness
--Believe in yourself, but do not become stifled by vanity
--Complacency will asphyxiate and stagnate you
--Compromise your integrity and begin the first step towards self-destruction
--Conceding your lack of knowledge is the first step toward a solid education
--Dig deep into yourself and witness possibilities springing forth from the well
--Do not be complicit in your own downfall
--Do not become intoxicated by the fumes of your success
--Don't be strangled by the urge to compete against others, challenge yourself, the most formidable competitor
--Don't dream of dreamers dreaming you
--Don't dwell on probabilities, but instead invest in the limitless possibilities
--Don't live trying to please your loved ones, but to better their lot
--Dwell on the past and be strangled by its tentacles of stagnation
--Educate yourself before you dare to assume the education of others
--Education begins within you
--Even the most dreaded curve in the road in the road of life, can lead you to a place where your dreams will be fulfilled
--Fail to recognize who you are and stumble on yourself in the darkness
--Faith ceases to be thus when effort and application reveal themselves
--Faith must not yield to pragmatism

--He/she who boasts of modesty tacitly admits arrogance

--He/she who shelters knowledge spreads ignorance

--Honor your family and in the process bring honor to yourself

--If you believe that education begins in the classroom, you have already begun the process of miseducation

--Inspire one person, then stand back and witness the magic of permutation at work

--Learn who you are by exploring the unchartered dimensions of yourself

--Listening is the centerpiece of the art of meaningful communication

--Lower the sound of arrogance to truly hear yourself

--Nature is recalling its own

--No truth greater than that which awakens your conscience

--One's greatest strength may well be the acknowledgment of his/her weaknesses

--Opportunity may not necessarily identify itself, introduce yourself to it

--Seek advice but ultimately listen to the voice from within

--Silence yourself before silencing others

--Silence yourself in order to hear yourself

--Tell who you are, less through words, but by the blueprint of your actions

--The first step of many steps may be unrecorded but it is the base for the later more heralded ones

--The individual who believes that he/she is "self-made" is delusional

--The loudest voice in the choir is not necessarily the best

--The most brilliant individual may well be she/he who brings out the brilliance in others

--The most deadly, ghastly fear, is the fear of oneself

--The only way to avert the atrocities of the past is to subvert the ideological traps securely set in history

--The stranger you fear may be yourself

--The suffering independent nation may well be in better shape than the overly dependent thriving state

--There is no such thing as a solo act

--Treat me royally and receive my gratitude, treat me fairly earn my respect

--Trust those who have proven their love through action; eye suspiciously those who only boast of it

---Wealth is defined as the reservoir of unbridled humanity embedded in your soul

---What is knowledge but the willingness to concede the lack of it?

--What is the past if not a barometer of the future?

--When the voice of reason and rationality is ignored, the door of anarchy and chaos automatically swings wide open

--Who are we? Coming from others who come from elsewhere who are coming from others coming from elsewhere?

--Your greatest benefits may well be those done for others

--Your mother, though gone, still is the rudder of the ship on this journey

--Your quest to comprehend the world must begin with your resolve to know yourself

===

Clement A. White, the son of Charles White and Marjorie Asta Stevens, is a native of St. Thomas, Virgin Islands, but spent a significant portion of his formative years on St. Croix, where his father was born and raised. He obtained his A.A. from the College of the Virgin Islands (now UVI), BA and MA degrees from Kent State University and his Ph.D. from Brown University. He is the author of: _Decoding the Word_; _Network of Spheres_; _Wey Butty: A Poetic Journey In Search of a West Indian Identity_, _Come Lemme Hea' Yoh Yank Soursap_; _Meet Meh Undah deh Bongolo & Tark Like We, No—A Case for Virgin Islands Creole Den an' Now & A Socio-cultural Lexicon, Bings Deh Quaksa & Other Stories_. He is also the author of various articles, including on Nicolás Guillén, Agustín Yáñez, and Langston Hughes. White is currently a Professor of Spanish/Latin American Literature at the University of Rhode Island where he has served as Director of the Graduate Program in Hispanic Studies from 1998 to 2017.

Printed in the United States
By Bookmasters